BUILT FOR SUCCESS

THE STORY OF

Microsoft

Published by Creative Education
P.O. Box 227, Mankato, Minnesota 56002
Creative Education is an imprint of The Creative Company.

DESIGN AND PRODUCTION BY **ZENO DESIGN**

Printed in the United States of America

PHOTOGRAPHS BY Alamy (Artpartner-images.com, Frank
Chmura, Dave Jepson, Ian Shaw, Vario Images GmbH & Co.
KG), Corbis (NATION BILL, Bettmann, Kevin P. Casey, Najlah
Feanny, Wolfgang Kaehler, Dan Lamont, Matthew Mcvay,
Jim Sugar, TWPhoto, Doug Wilson, Naashon Zalk), Getty
Images (China Photos, Sam Forencich/NBA, Joe McNally,
Diana Walker/Liaison, Ron Wurzer)

LIBRARY OF CONGRESS CATALOGING-IN-PUBLICATION DATA

Musolf, Nell.
The story of Microsoft / by Nell Musolf.
p. cm. — (Built for success)
Includes index
ISBN-13: 978-1-58341-607-5
1. Microsoft Corporation—History—Juvenile literature. 2.
Computer software industry—United States—History—
Juvenile literature. I. Title.

HD9696.63.U64M5346 2008
338.7'610050973—dc22   2007014994

9 8 7 6 5 4 3

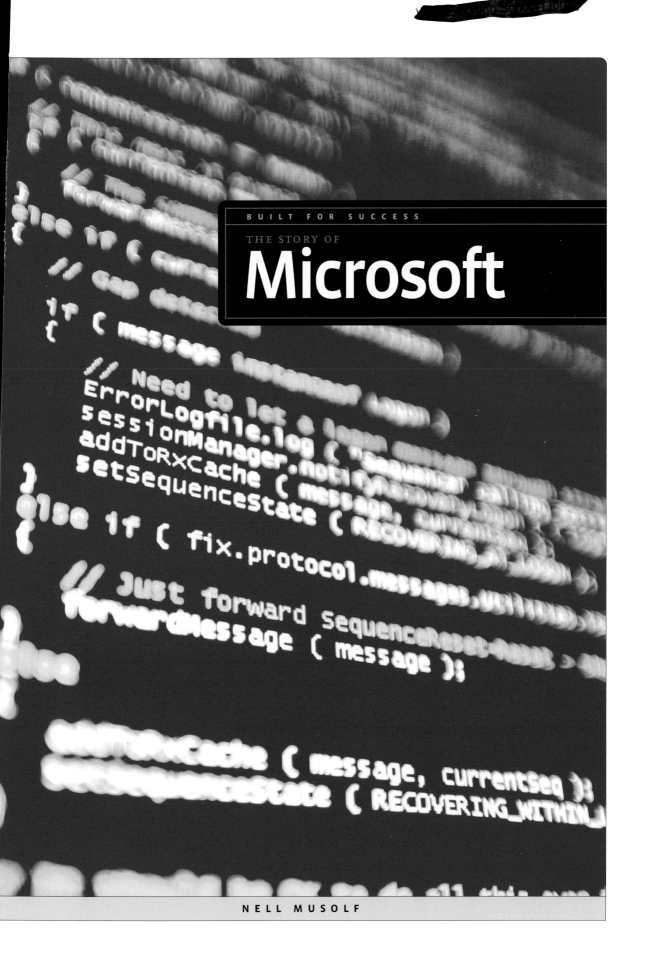

BUILT FOR SUCCESS

THE STORY OF

Microsoft

NELL MUSOLF

Microsoft software architect Ray Ozzie

E spresso stations in every office building. Private offices where workers are encouraged to merely "sit and think," free of distractions. The faint hum of computers filling the air. Such is everyday life in Redmond, Washington, at the headquarters of Microsoft Corporation, a giant in the world of computing software. Since it was founded in 1975, Microsoft has become one of the most famous and successful companies in the world. Through its innovative, user-friendly software, Microsoft was one of the pioneers responsible for bringing the personal computer into the lives of millions of people. The company's impact has been such that the name "Microsoft" is now virtually synonymous with computer software—and it all began three decades ago with two young men who were captivated by computers.

CHAPTER ONE

The Early Days

Although computers were being built and used as early as the 1930s, they didn't enter the modern age until the 1960s. The first personal computers of the early '60s did not have much in common with personal computers of today. Those early machines were bulky, heavy, expensive, and used primarily by businesses, hospitals, and large universities that could afford them.

Since they did not have their own computers, it was common practice for small schools to rent computer time from larger schools or colleges. In 1967, at Lakeside School, a private middle and high school in the Seattle, Washington, area, the Lakeside Mothers Club held a fundraiser to rent computer time for the students. After raising $3,000, the club members thought they would be able to purchase ample computer time for the entire student body. But they hadn't counted on the interest of two seventh-grade students named Kent Evans and Bill Gates. Fascinated by computers ever since a math teacher had taken them to see the school's ASR-33 Teletype, a machine used to send typed messages from one point to another electronically, Evans and Gates spent all the time they could on the computer the

Although fairly simplistic, the Teletype electronic typewriter fascinated Kent Evans and Bill Gates

Lakeside Mothers Club had leased for them. The $3,000 worth of computer time was quickly consumed.

Evans and Gates soon formed the Lakeside Programmers Club, a group devoted to writing computer programs. They were joined by Paul Allen and Rick Weiland, two high school students who were also intrigued by computers. The Lakeside Programmers Club landed several jobs for the young **entrepreneurs** that included developing a payroll system for a local business and computerizing their own school's class schedules.

One day, while working at the computer, Gates remarked to Allen, "Don't you think that someday everybody will have one of these things? And if they did, couldn't you deliver magazines and newspapers and stuff through them?" His comment was a remarkably accurate prediction of the future of the personal computer.

Throughout their years at Lakeside School, Allen and Gates spent as much time as they could working on computers, becoming good friends in the process. After the tragic death of Kent Evans in a mountain climbing accident, their friendship grew stronger. It was the beginning of a lifelong partnership that would eventually become one of the biggest successes in the history of American business.

In 1969, a general-purpose **computer chip** was invented by Ted Hoff, a researcher at the Intel Corporation. With the invention, which enabled computers to be built more quickly and cheaply, personal computers took a major step forward in becoming more accessible to the average consumer.

Six years later, the January 1975 issue of *Popular Electronics* magazine featured the Altair 8800, calling it the world's "first minicomputer." In truth, the Altair was more of an electronic hobby kit than a computer. For $397, the kit could be purchased through the mail and assembled at home. When completed, the Altair was a metal box with flashing lights and switches, and there wasn't much to do with it other than play tic-tac-toe. But that didn't matter to

Bill Gates (left) and Paul Allen (right), shown here in 1983, were obsessed with computers in high school

computer enthusiasts. In just one afternoon, MITS (Micro Instrumentation and Telemetry Systems), the company that made the Altair, took 400 orders for the computer. In three weeks, the company earned $250,000.

Allen spotted the issue of *Popular Electronics* one day on his way to visit Gates at Harvard University, where Gates was then a student. At the time, Allen was working for Honeywell, an electronics company. From their years of study and experimentation, Allen and Gates were well acquainted with the two principle parts of a computer: the **hardware** and software. Hardware refers to the physical parts, or the mechanics, of the computer. Software includes the programs that run the computer, or tell the hardware what to do. After reading the article on the Altair 8800, the two friends agreed that the growing world of personal computers was going to need a great deal of software.

Allen and Gates contacted MITS owner Ed Roberts in 1975. They told him that they'd created an easy-to-use computer language based on a 1960s general-purpose programming language called BASIC (Beginner's All-purpose Symbolic Instruction Code), and that their program would enable the Altair 8800 to interpret the BASIC language program. What Allen and Gates told Roberts wasn't completely true; they hadn't actually written their version of BASIC yet, but they were confident that they could. Roberts agreed to try their program. In less than five weeks, working around the clock, Allen and Gates finished their version of BASIC. It became known as Altair BASIC.

When the Altair BASIC program was completed, Allen flew to Albuquerque, New Mexico, where MITS was located. All of the time and work that Allen and Gates had put into Altair BASIC paid off. Altair BASIC was efficient and easy to use, giving users increased memory and the familiarity of the BASIC computer language. After seeing how well Altair BASIC worked, MITS offered Allen a job, and in March 1975, he left his position at Honeywell and moved to Albuquerque. Gates remained at Harvard but kept in close contact with Allen. With the success of Altair BASIC, Allen and Gates planned to continue their partnership in the burgeoning world of computer software.

> "I was probably the one always pushing a little in terms of new technology and new products, and Bill [Gates] was more interested in doing negotiations and contracts and business deals."
>
> PAUL ALLEN, ON MICROSOFT'S BEGINNING

The DEC PDP-8 Microcomputer

Digital Equipment Corporation introduced the PDP family of minicomputers in the 1960s. As classmates, Bill Gates and Paul Allen convinced a local computer company to give them free access to its PDP in exchange for finding flaws in the system.

The Altair 8800 offered Bill Gates and Paul Allen a chance to devise their own computer language

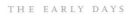

Chinese police examining pirated software

A LETTER TO HOBBYISTS

When Paul Allen and Bill Gates sold their version of BASIC to MITS in 1975, they signed a licensing agreement which stated that they would make money from the sale of their software if it was sold as part of the Altair or if it was sold separately. Gates in particular was concerned about the possibility of software copying by hobbyists, a practice known as "pirating." In "An Open Letter to Hobbyists," published in *Computer Notes* magazine in 1976, Gates argued that copying software was akin to stealing it and that software developers needed the protection of copyright laws similar to the laws that protected songwriters. The letter didn't have a large effect on computer users, and no copyright laws were created at that time. Computer users still seemed to prefer "borrowing" software from each other instead of buying their own copies, a problem Microsoft eventually addressed by increasing security measures on all of its software.

CHAPTER TWO

The Rise of Microsoft

After completing his second year of college, Gates went to Albuquerque for the summer in 1975. It was then that he and Allen decided to start their own computer software company. They originally called their company Micro-Soft but a few months later dropped the hyphen, and the company became known as Microsoft. Gates returned to Harvard that fall but left in 1977 before graduating to devote himself full-time to Microsoft.

Allen and Gates weren't the only people seeking new ways to improve personal computers. In 1976, Steve Jobs and Steve Wozniak, two young computer hobbyists from Palo Alto, California, unveiled the **prototype** for the Apple I computer. A local computer dealer saw the Apple I and ordered 100 pre-assembled units. Over the next 10 months, about 200 Apple I's were sold.

One year later, Jobs and Wozniak introduced the Apple II personal computer. The Apple II was sold already assembled, with 4 kilobytes (k) of **RAM**, or memory. It was simple to operate and featured color **graphics**, something no other personal computer had at that time. But, like all computers, the Apple II needed software. Jobs and Wozniak wanted to include software, such as games and word-processing

Steve Jobs's development of Apple Computer in the late 1970s created software opportunities for Microsoft

MICROSOFT

with a copy of Applesoft BASIC installed.

In 1978, Allen and Gates decided to move Microsoft from Albuquerque to the Pacific Northwest, where they'd both grown up. The next year, Microsoft—then made up of Gates, Allen, and nine other staff members—moved its headquarters to Bellevue, Washington.

In 1980, Steve Ballmer joined Microsoft as first assistant to president Bill Gates. Prior to moving to Microsoft, Ballmer had worked at Proctor and Gamble, a consumer products company, as an assistant project manager. A friend of Gates from their days at Harvard, Ballmer took over many of the administrative chores Gates had been handling.

Also in 1980, Allen and Gates donned business suits and ties instead of their usual jeans and casual shirts to discuss a possible contract with the International Business Machines (IBM) Company. IBM needed software to provide language and operating systems, or software that enabled the operation of various other programs, for its first personal computers. After securing the contract, Microsoft was suddenly the supplier of vital software to a giant in the computer industry. To meet IBM's needs, Gates and Allen created MS-DOS (Microsoft Disk Operating System) from a language named Q-DOS that they had purchased from the Seattle Computer Products company. In a move considered questionable by some, Microsoft didn't tell Seattle Computer Products about its impending deal with IBM. Instead, it simply said it had a customer that needed a program similar to Q-DOS. Microsoft then negotiated with IBM to retain separate **marketing** rights for the operating system. Q-DOS became PC-DOS for IBM, while MS-DOS was Microsoft's version.

> *"Our first major row came when I insisted it was time to hire 17 people. He [Bill Gates] claimed I was trying to bankrupt him."*
>
> MICROSOFT PRESIDENT STEVE BALLMER,
> ON HIS EARLY DAYS AT MICROSOFT

Hundreds of thousands of computers were sold in the early '80s, and a copy of MS-DOS was sold along with almost every one. Microsoft had become the crucial connection between the hardware and software needed to operate computers. The huge sales of MS-DOS fueled Microsoft's financial growth, increasing the company's annual revenue from $16 million in 1981 to $24.5 million in 1982.

February 1983 marked a big change at Microsoft. After learning that he had Hodgkin's disease, a kind of cancer, Paul Allen resigned from his position as executive vice president of Microsoft. "To be 30 years old and have that kind of shock—to face your own mortality—makes you feel like you should do some of the things that you haven't done," Allen said. After successful medical treatment, Allen remained on the board of directors at Microsoft but stepped down permanently from daily operations, choosing instead to devote his time to other interests beyond computers, such as sailing and various **philanthropic** endeavors.

Another important event unfolded in 1983. When Steve Jobs told Microsoft about Apple's newest technology, the Macintosh computer, or the "Mac," Microsoft signed a contract with Apple to develop software programs that could run on the Macintosh. Gates asked his researchers to develop a **GUI**, or **graphical user interface**, that could be used on IBM-compatible machines as well. That way, Microsoft stood to make a profit by providing software systems for both Apple and IBM computers.

The Macintosh was simple to use and popular with consumers, but in 1983, IBM was still the largest and most important company in the computer hardware industry. Since IBM had chosen to use Microsoft's software, other hardware companies, such as Tandy and Commodore, also chose to use Microsoft. To keep up with their expanding list of clients, Microsoft soon hired more programmers, managers, and office support staff, increasing Microsoft's payroll to 476 employees in 1983 as annual sales passed $50 million.

> "Bill [Gates] has done a great job of cloning himself as the company has grown. Now there are all these aggressive 'Little Bills'… and they keep coming at you and coming at you."
>
> STEVE JOBS, APPLE COMPUTER EXECUTIVE

Paul Allen made various investments after 1983; in 2003, he financed the history-making private spacecraft *SpaceShipOne*

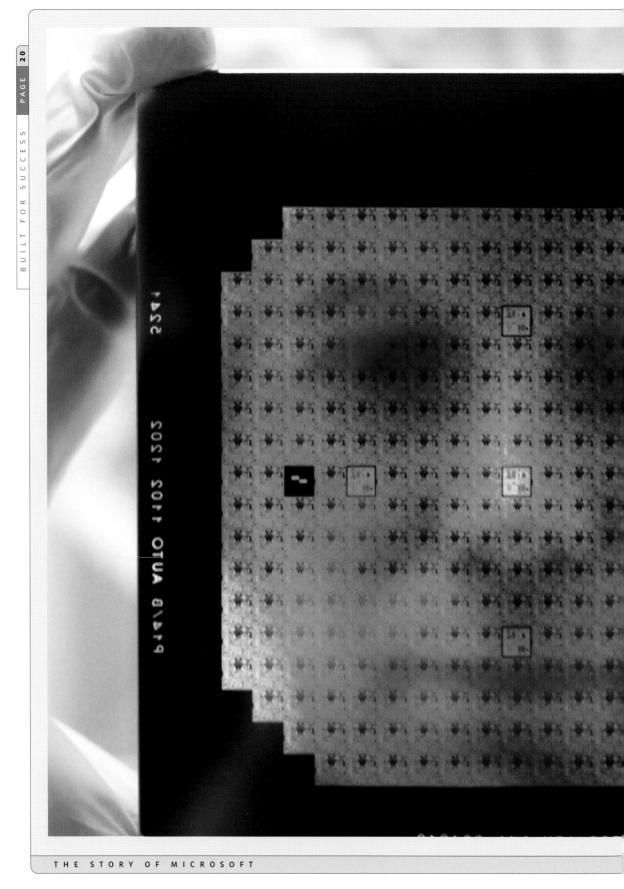

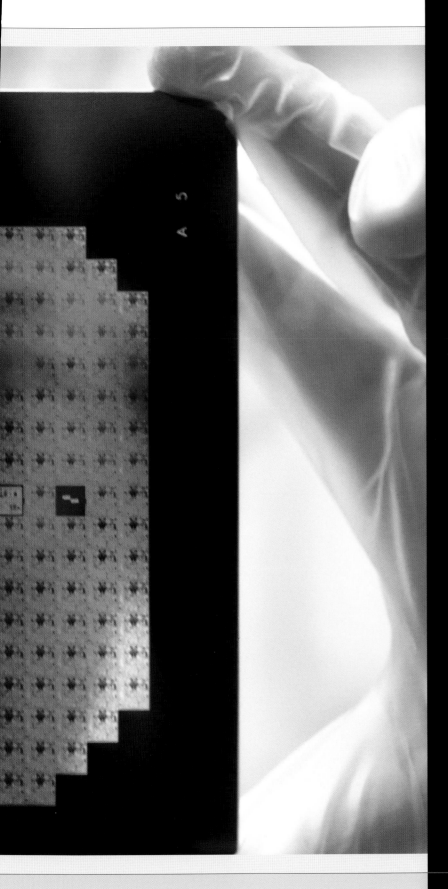

COMPUTER IN A CHIP

When Intel researcher Ted Hoff invented the first **silicon** computer chip in 1969, it was a major step toward putting computers into not just offices, but homes as well. Computer chips are tiny pieces of material, typically silicon, that contain an electronic circuit. The two major types of computer chips are microprocessors, which carry out the instructions of a computer program, and memory chips, which hold programs and information. Microprocessor chips are used in computers, video games, digital watches, microwave ovens, and certain types of telephones. Memory chips are divided into two categories: ones with read-only memory (ROM), and ones with random-access memory (RAM). ROM chips hold on to their memory even when the computer is turned off. RAM chips hold their memory only as long as the computer has power. Without computer chips, personal computers might never have been invented, and companies such as Microsoft might not exist.

CHAPTER THREE

Windows to the World

L ate in 1983, Microsoft introduced its most advanced word-processing program to date, Microsoft Word, and also announced the creation of a program called Windows, which would be released in 1985. Windows was a true innovation in the computer world, as it allowed users to open more than one document at the same time.

Microsoft's computer **mouse**, similar to the Mac's mouse, was another new item. The mouse let people simply point at and click on an onscreen command instead of typing in lines of commands, thus reducing keystrokes and work time.

But in spite of its innovative features, Windows received negative reviews from users. Microsoft had hurried its programmers to finish Windows and get it on the market as quickly as possible. As a result, Windows had significant limitations—for example, open documents, or "windows," could not overlap one another on the screen—and used up a great deal of computer memory, causing computers to freeze, or "crash." Microsoft programmers were compelled to go back into Windows and repair the problems.

In addition to being faulted for rushing a product into stores before it was ready, Microsoft also found itself accused of indulging in a marketing tactic known in the computer world as "vaporware." Vaporware refers to a ploy by which a company

With the introduction of Windows, Bill Gates helped change computer history by making multitasking simple

announces a product well before it is ready to be sold to consumers. By practicing vaporware, Microsoft could discourage potential customers from buying a competitor's product before Microsoft's product was available, such as when Microsoft announced the pending arrival of the first Windows well before the product was complete. Microsoft was also occasionally charged with buying out their competitors' products from stores so that customers had no choice but to purchase a Microsoft product, an allegation that Microsoft denied.

In the summer of 1985, construction began on new corporate headquarters—soon to become known as Microsoft Place—in Redmond, Washington. The casual, relaxed atmosphere at Microsoft Place and the young age of most of the employees led many people to compare it to a college campus. Set in a wooded area, buildings were designed in an X shape to receive the maximum amount of sunlight. Consisting of 41 buildings and covering 270 acres (109 ha), the complex also had walking paths and a softball field for programmers and office personnel to use when they needed a break. A large pond in the middle of the grounds was dubbed "Lake Bill" in honor of the company's president.

Microsoft celebrated its 10th year in business in 1985. Over that decade, Microsoft had grown into a major corporation that employed 900 people and enjoyed annual sales of $140 million. By 1986, Microsoft had increased its employee ranks to 1,153, and its **stock** went public, meaning people outside the company were allowed to became part-owners. The first day the stock went on the market, Microsoft earned $61 million. Within one year, 31-year-old Bill Gates would be a billionaire.

Windows 2.0 was launched in 1987, an event that marked the beginning of a legal battle with Apple Computer. The previously friendly relationship Microsoft and Apple had enjoyed changed when, in 1988, Apple brought a lawsuit against Microsoft, claiming that the idea for Windows had been taken from Apple's designs. Microsoft countered that both Windows and Mac systems used different features taken from the same source: Xerox's Alto computer. Xerox didn't sell

The vast Microsoft Place, which opened in 1986, today accommodates more than 30,000 Microsoft employees

its computer system, so the features it used could be integrated by any company. Apple then brought a second lawsuit against Microsoft which claimed that Microsoft had illegally copied aspects—such as its rectangular boxes containing commands—of Macintosh's operating system. Microsoft would ultimately win both cases in federal court in 1992.

Microsoft's relationship with IBM was also troubled in 1988. Microsoft designed a software package called OS/2 for IBM at the same time Windows 2.0 was created, causing IBM to worry that Windows 2.0 would take customers away from OS/2. IBM's fears were realized when Windows 2.0 outsold IBM's OS/2 by a wide margin, not because OS/2 wasn't technically sound but because, many people believed, of Microsoft's effective marketing for Windows 2.0.

Windows 3.0 was completed and released in 1990 with the largest marketing campaign in Microsoft's history. It was a hit with computer users from the moment it came on the market, due primarily to a major redesign that included larger memory support as well as a more colorful user interface. Windows 3.0 was so profitable that Microsoft became, in 1990, the first computer software company ever to top $1 billion in sales. "Windows, Windows, Windows!" Steve Ballmer chanted at company meetings as the software program sold 100,000 copies during its first two weeks on the market. Microsoft would continue cheering as it became—and remained—the world's undisputed leader in software throughout the 1990s.

The success of Windows 3.0 only riled IBM further, and IBM renewed its accusations that Microsoft intentionally hadn't put as much effort into the programs it designed for IBM so that Windows 3.0 would win a bigger share of the market. Also, Windows 3.0 wasn't compatible with OS/2, so people who chose to use Windows 3.0 wouldn't be able to work on an IBM computer. More lawsuits were leveled against Microsoft. It wouldn't be the last time the company would be accused of not dealing fairly with competitors.

IBM, the world's largest computer company, and Microsoft have had an up-and-down relationship

As Microsoft became phenom-
enally successful, Bill Gates and
his wife, Melinda, became philan-
thropists and created the Bill and
Melinda Gates Foundation. While
the Foundation has both local and
global goals, it strives primarily to
reduce poverty, improve health
care, and help educate people every-
where. The Foundation believes that
through science and technology, people's lives can be improved. Since it
was founded in 1999, it has created
grant commitments, or promises of
money, of $11 billion. In 2005, total
grant payments reached $1.36 billion.
By applying scientific and technolog-
ical innovations—such as supplying
vaccines to help prevent common
childhood diseases—the Foundation
helps the world's neediest people. As
the Gateses state on their foundation's Web site, "We ... believe that
from those to whom much is given,
much is expected. We benefited from
great schools, great health care, and
a vibrant economic system. That is
why we feel a tremendous responsi-
bility to give back to society."

CHAPTER FOUR

The Age of the Internet

The 1990s ushered in another period of growth at Microsoft. In 1991, Microsoft introduced the Microsoft Ballpoint Mouse, a mouse designed to work with **laptop computers**. The Microsoft Ballpoint Mouse clamped onto the side of the computer and used no desk space, allowing users to easily navigate a computer screen any time, anywhere.

Two years later, Microsoft Encarta, a multimedia encyclopedia that contained all the information of a traditional set of encyclopedias on one **CD-ROM**, was unveiled. Another 1993 innovation was the Mouse 2.0, a new mouse designed for comfortable use by both left-handed and right-handed users. The year ended with *Fortune* magazine naming Microsoft the "Most Innovative Company Working in the United States."

By 1995, as Microsoft celebrated its 20th anniversary, the company had grown to more than 16,350 employees. In August of that year, Windows 95 was released to great fanfare. Windows 95, with its easy installation and ability to be customized to the individual user, promised to outperform all previous versions of Windows. Microsoft promoted its latest Windows with parties, television commercials, and major media events; the famous Empire State Building in New York City, for example,

Whether on T-shirts or the Empire State Building, Windows 95 was a big news story in August 1995

was illuminated in the red, green, blue, and yellow colors of the Windows logo. The advertising strategy worked; after just four days on the market, more than one million copies of Windows 95 had been sold in North America. More than seven million copies were sold worldwide by October.

Microsoft leaped into the Internet age by rolling out the Microsoft Network (MSN), a full-service Internet provider, in 1995. Three months after its launch, the network had more than 500,000 members. Later that same year, Microsoft introduced a new version of MSN named Microsoft Internet Explorer, which was a more advanced Internet **browser**. Before 1995 ended, Microsoft, along with the NBC television network, had created a new 24-hour news channel called MSNBC and a corresponding online news service.

A reunion occurred between Microsoft and Apple in 1997. In spite of the difficulties the two companies had encountered in the past, they came to the realization that they could make better products working together than they could working apart. Under the new arrangement, Microsoft would produce future versions of Microsoft Office, Internet Explorer, and other tools for the Macintosh, and the two companies would share a wide **patent** and **cross-licensing** agreement. Microsoft would also invest $150 million in Apple, while Apple would make Microsoft's Internet Explorer the **default** browser link to the Internet on its new computers.

In 1998, a change occurred in the corporate structure at Microsoft when Steve Ballmer was appointed president. Gates, the former president, remained chairman and chief executive officer (CEO) of Microsoft. Microsoft also made news in 1998 when its Internet Explorer sparked one of the biggest lawsuits in the history of American business.

The lawsuit came about when the U.S. Department of Justice alleged that Microsoft had broken **antitrust laws**. When Microsoft created its Windows 98 operating system, the Microsoft Internet Explorer browser came automatically with any computer that ran on the Windows operating system. The U.S.

Microsoft leaped into the world of the Internet in the mid-1990s with the Microsoft Network and Internet Explorer

Department of Justice believed that, by including Microsoft Internet Explorer with its software packages, Microsoft was trying to force other browser companies out of the market. It was hard for smaller companies, such as Netscape and the fledgling America Online (AOL), to compete in the Internet browser market because Microsoft's product was sold with so many computers. The Justice Department also claimed that Microsoft was close to having a **monopoly** and had used its power to force Internet service providers into exclusive deals using Microsoft Internet Explorer.

In response to these charges, Microsoft asserted that it was largely responsible for the Internet revolution of the 1990s, a revolution that had been highly beneficial for the U.S. economy. In order to reduce Microsoft's enormous clout in the software world, the government recommended that it include other browsers, such as Netscape and AOL, along with Internet Explorer in its software packages. Not surprisingly, this suggestion was not popular among Microsoft executives. "It would be like asking Coca-Cola to ship three Pepsis with every six-pack," one remarked after hearing the government's idea.

Microsoft defended itself by claiming that it had planned to include Internet Explorer with its software packages before Netscape and other companies were even founded. Company officials said that computer manufacturers included Internet Explorer on their systems because it was a good browser program, not because Microsoft forced them to do so. "Our success is based on only one thing: good products," said Gates. "It's not very complicated. We're not powerful enough to cause products that are not excellent to sell well."

In spite of the company's legal problems, the 20th century ended on a high note for Microsoft. In March 1999, Internet Explorer 5.0 was introduced. Within one week, more than one million consumers had **downloaded** the new version. As the millennium drew to a close, Microsoft had more than 30,000 employees and a **net income** of $7.79 billion.

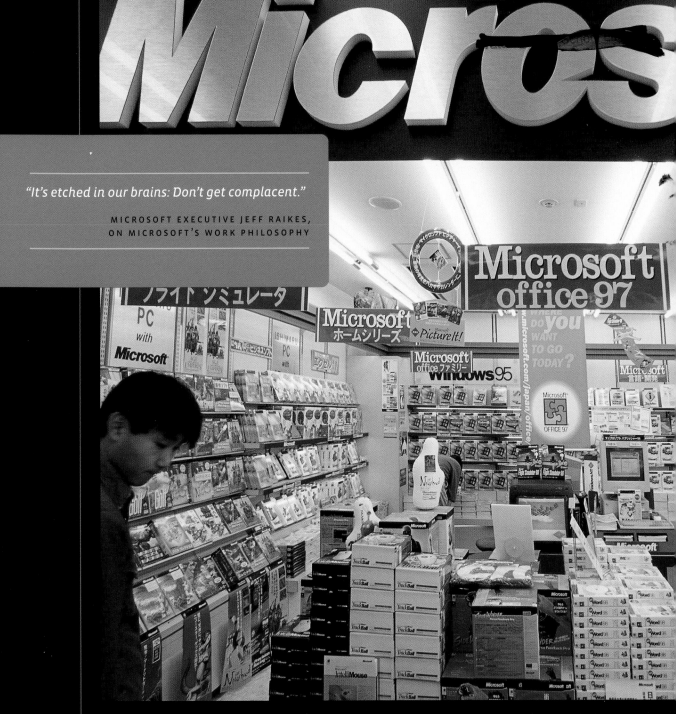

Microsoft has been accused of violating antitrust laws—in the U.S. and abroad—since the late 1990s.

LIFE AT MICROSOFT

In some ways, the Microsoft work-place is more relaxed and casual than the environment one might find at other corporations. But the computer programmers, office administrators, and other personnel employed by Microsoft know that they are working for bosses who expect the best. Microsoft employees work hard and put in long hours, but they're rewarded with lavish holiday parties and company picnics every summer. They're also rewarded with the knowledge that, thanks to stock options, the company they work for has more millionaires on the payroll than any other corporation in the world. But Microsoft employees are aware of the fact that they're expected to follow certain rules. "If you're going to work for this company, you're going to rent a certain kind of hotel room and fly coach, because that's business and anything else is luxury," explained Microsoft president and CEO Steve Ballmer.

CHAPTER FIVE

Microsoft and the New Millennium

Microsoft finally reached an agreement with the Justice Department over the antitrust lawsuit in 2001. According to the terms of the settlement, Microsoft had to permit a panel of three independent monitors to work at the Microsoft campus with full access to the company's records and personnel for five years.

The company also had to provide other software companies, such as Netscape, with information that allowed them to develop programs that interacted with Microsoft operating systems as easily as Microsoft's own products. Microsoft also agreed to donate money, in the form of software, computers, and training, to more than 12,500 schools.

In the early years of the new millennium, Microsoft entered a new dimension of the computer industry: video games. In the 1980s, electronic games had been designed to be downloaded and played on personal computers. Sony's PlayStation, introduced in 1995, was a console designed strictly for game-playing, and its success and lucrative profits compelled Microsoft to jump into the business.

When Microsoft unveiled the high-powered Xbox gaming system in 2001, the console was an immediate hit with consumers. An online gaming experience called Xbox Live soon let gamers from all over the world link up and play multiplayer

Microsoft agreed to make donations to schools as part of the 2001 antitrust lawsuit settlement

games and tournaments against one another. In 2005, Microsoft introduced the more powerful Xbox 360 system, which featured the most intense and graphically realistic games yet. "There has never been a more exciting time to be a gamer," Microsoft noted in a press release when Xbox 360 came out. "Xbox 360 will deliver mind-blowing experiences across multiple **genres**, no matter what your personal gaming preferences are." Microsoft's science-fiction combat game *Halo* and its sequels were especially popular and critically acclaimed games.

Microsoft continued fighting legal battles as the new millennium progressed. Most of the lawsuits brought against Microsoft were about the same thing: how Microsoft dominated the computer software market, often to the detriment of smaller companies. In many instances, Microsoft was able to settle the lawsuits out of court, thereby avoiding expensive trials and negative publicity. Yet Microsoft's common practice of donating software as part of its out-of-court settlements seemed to serve a double purpose to critics who pointed out that, in addition to bringing positive publicity to Microsoft, Microsoft also made sure that the schools receiving their software wouldn't buy the competitors' software instead.

In June 2006, Microsoft announced that Bill Gates would be leaving his position as chief software architect, a title he'd held since 2000, to devote more time to his work at the Bill and Melinda Gates Foundation, a philanthropic organization created in 1999 by Gates and his wife Melinda. Gates stated that he planned to continue as chairman and adviser of Microsoft. "I'm very lucky to have two passions that I feel are so important and so challenging. As I prepare for change, I firmly believe the road ahead for Microsoft is as bright as ever," Gates said upon announcing his decision. Chief technical officer Ray Ozzie took over as Microsoft's chief software architect.

Microsoft's other founder, Paul Allen, had also stayed busy since leaving full-time duties at Microsoft in 1983, finding success with his investments in real estate and professional sports teams, and filling much of his time with

By 2007, six years after launching the Xbox, Microsoft had become a heavyweight in the world of video gaming

philanthropic works. Through his charitable organization, the Paul G. Allen Family Foundation, he had, by 2003, donated more than $43 billion to a wide variety of global causes, including education, the arts, and scientific research.

As Gates prepared to leave the daily corporate world in 2006, Microsoft announced the release of its latest version of Windows, called Vista. With a new design, easier search and organization tools, and the promise of a safer online experience, Vista was the most heavily tested operating system to date. Microsoft believed Windows Vista would become the standard by which all operating systems would be measured.

Microsoft made another splash in the computer gaming industry in 2007 with the introduction of IPTV, or Internet Protocol Television, on Xbox 360. IPTV on Xbox 360 delivered digital video recording capabilities with gaming, movie viewing, and voice and video communications. "Our goal is to make entertainment more personal, more interactive, and more social," said Microsoft Entertainment and Devices Division president Robbie Bach. "We are bringing together the worlds of gaming, TV viewing, and community to make it easy for people to ... share their personal experiences with the community they are a part of."

The world of personal computers has evolved a great deal, and at breakneck speed, since 1975, when Paul Allen and Bill Gates founded Microsoft in Albuquerque, New Mexico. From the days of playing tic-tac-toe on the Altair to the modern high-speed office applications of Vista, change has been the one constant in the world of computers. Through good times and bad, Microsoft has shown a rare ability to see those changes coming and, indeed, bring many of those changes about—an ability that has made it one of the true giants in the business world today.

"*Microsoft is not about greed. It's about innovation and fairness.*"

BILL GATES

Showing its typical flair for product introduction, Microsoft made headlines in 2006 with its newest Windows program

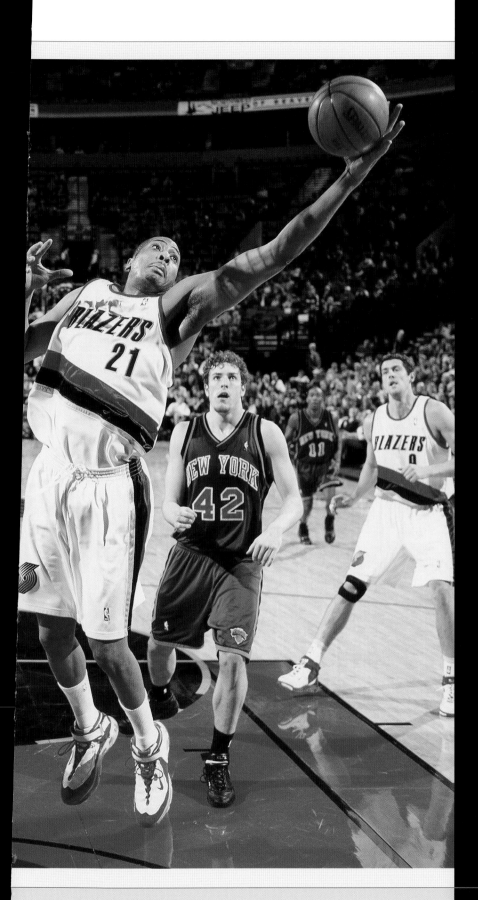

THE RICH LIFE

Bill Gates and Paul Allen are two of the wealthiest people in the world. While they both donate generously to a wide variety of charitable causes, they know how to enjoy the billions of dollars they've earned, too. Allen owns the Portland Trail Blazers professional basketball team (since 1988) and the Seattle Seahawks pro football team (since 1997). He also owns a yacht that carries two helicopters and a submarine. Gates used a portion of his wealth to build a palatial house on Lake Washington in Medina, Washington, close to Microsoft's headquarters. The 40,000-square-foot (3,716 sq m) house has a 30-car garage, a swimming pool with an underwater sound system, a movie theater, and a dining room that seats 150 guests. Gates also collects art and antiques. In 1994, he bought the Codex Leicester, a 72-page notebook that belonged to artist Leonardo da Vinci, for $30.8 million.

GLOSSARY

applications software that runs specific types of computer programs; examples include word processors and music-playing programs

antitrust laws laws that protect companies from unfair business practices, such as one company gaining total control of a certain market

browser a program that allows a computer user to look through a collection of data, typically on the Internet; examples include Netscape and Internet Explorer

CD-ROM a computer disk that contains information that can be read but not changed; ROM stands for "Read-Only Memory"

computer chip an electronic circuit that is a basic component of many electronic devices

cross-licensing the sharing of patents between two or more companies

default automatic action that is taken if other instructions are not given or received

downloaded copied, as data, to a computer (usually from an online, or Internet, source)

entrepreneurs people who start or organize a business of their own

genres distinctive types or categories

graphics displays generated by a computer on a screen or printer; graphics may include text, images, or other visual displays

GUI (graphical user interface) a visual display on a screen that enables users to connect and interact with their computers

hardware the physical parts of a computer, such as the central processing unit, disks, modem, and cables

laptop computers small, lightweight computers that are designed to be portable and can be easily held on the user's lap

marketing advertising and promoting a product in order to increase sales

mouse a small device that controls the movement of an arrow, or pointer, on a computer screen; it assists in moving things on the screen or giving computer commands

monopoly exclusive control by one group over a commercial activity

net income the total income a company has after subtracting costs and expenses from total revenues

patent an official document that says who has the right to use, make, or sell an invention

philanthropic describing a person or organization who supports charitable causes through financial donations; the term also describes such efforts

prototype an original model that other, later copies are based upon

RAM (Random-Access Memory) memory chips that can be used by programs while a computer is in use

silicon a nonmetallic chemical that is commonly used to make certain computer parts

software the programs that run a computer, or tell it how to operate

stock shared ownership in a company by many people who buy shares, or portions, of stock, hoping the company will make a profit and the stock value will increase

SELECTED BIBLIOGRAPHY

Campbell-Kelly, Martin, and William Aspray. *Computer: A History of the Information Machine.* New York: BasicBooks, 1996.

Gates, Bill. *Business @ the Speed of Thought.* New York: Warner Books, 1999.

The Microsoft Corporation. "Homepage." http://www.microsoft.com.

Raatma, Lucia. *Bill Gates: Computer Programmer and Entrepreneur.* Chicago: Ferguson Publishing Company, 2000.

Wukovits, John. *Bill Gates: Software King.* New York: Franklin Watts, 2000.

INDEX